BIOGRAPHY

OF THE

HON. SOLOMON W. DOWNS,

OF LOUISIANA.

BY A LOUISIANIAN.

Printed by Robert Armstrong.

PREFACE.

The writer of the biographical sketch which is to follow approaches the task he has voluntarily undertaken with no little pleasure. This is because the eventful public life of his subject is replete with facts bearing upon the progress of a great State of this Union, in the adoption of improvements in her laws and institutions founded in the root of American liberty and national and social progress—the political principles of Thomas Jefferson. To him it is, indeed, a pleasure to contemplate the career of Senator Downs, which, in his mind's eye, presents a faithful type of the gradual verging of our country's institutions to that condition of universal political equality among its citizens, and all who should be its citizens, to which Thomas Jefferson looked forward as the ultimate result of the operation of his views of government, when carried out in spirit and in truth.

The yoke of special privilege—that old man of the sea upon all people who would be free in fact as in name—descended to us legitimately. In parting from the thraldom of our mother—England—we rid ourselves of little more than our immediate government. Many of the principles of the constitution were fixed in the hearts of our fathers, as to this hour not a few of the most odious features of her laws are still upon American statute-books. Mr. Jefferson and his compeers in their day, laying out the plan of battle, commenced the struggle against the ascendency of both, which has been prosecuted by their disciples with more or less good fortune, and none with more vigor and success than by the subject of our notice; for he has been to the State of Louisiana what Andrew Jackson was to the United States—the destroyer of a monstrous scheme of special privileges under the guise of irresponsible and corrupt banking corporations, which, while industriously appropriating to themselves the proceeds of the labor of the people of the State, lost no opportunity, by example and the doctrines they caused to be promulgated in their justification, to sap the business morals of the community. As a democrat, I honor any man who has made a General Jackson sort of a fight against corrupt banks. This, however, was but a third of the task which history proves to have been that marked out for himself by Senator Downs early in his career as a statesman—the extension of the right of suffrage and the reform of the judiciary of his State completing his labor of love for the principles of equal rights. In all these he was eminently successful, as the reader will in the end perceive. The contemplation of his marked features, as traced upon the plate in the Democratic Review, will strike all true-hearted republicans that he is indeed a reformer on principle—a man of deep thought, far-seeing sagacity, unyielding views of the fitness of things, ardent devotion to what he regards as the cause of right, courage to defend that cause against any and all odds, and industry knowing no point at which to flag short of the attainment of his object. Such, emphatically, has Senator Downs proved himself to be, in the crucible of perhaps the fiercest and longest struggle for reform which has distinguished the political progress of any State of this Union.

PHILADELPHIA, *May* 4, 1852.

BIOGRAPHY.

Solomon W. Downs was born in 1801, in Tennessee. When a boy he emigrated to Louisiana, from whence he was sent to Tennessee, where he received his academical education under the tuition of the late Rev. T. Craighead, the early associate and fast friend of Andrew Jackson, who in his day was the most renowned instructor of youth in the State. When fit for college he was entered in Transylvania University, where, after pursuing the usual course of studies under the immediate supervision of the celebrated Dr. Holley, he graduated. Among his academical fellow-students were the late Richard Winn, since a lawyer of distinguished abilities and a State senator for the parish of Rapides in the Louisiana legislature; William H. Wharton, the pioneer of the Texas revolution, who first represented the young republic as minister to the United States; the talented and intrepid brother of the latter—the late John A. Wharton; Frederick Guion, late of the United States army—one of the most gifted sons of the South; and Judges John J. Guion, of Vicksburg, Mississippi; and Felix Bosworth, of Louisiana—all of whom have made their respective marks upon the history of the times in which they lived.

At one period since General Downs has served the State of Louisiana in the United States Senate, four of his fellow-senators had been his college mates at Transylvania University. They were Messrs. Atchison, Hannegan, Jefferson Davis, and Jones of Iowa. This, I believe, is the only instance on record where such a number of the graduates of a collegiate institution studying together have served at one time in the Congress of the United States. I recur to it, more particularly to show that the attraction of mind in the ordinary collegiate intercourse of such college mates must have done much in the way of early developing their intellectual powers. After graduating at the university, General Downs commenced the study of the law; and on being admitted to the practice, according to the custom of the South, he soon found himself involved in politics. In 1828, his political speeches and writings began to attract attention, marking him for a rising public man, likely to be of real service to the State. He took an active part in the canvass of that year in favor of General Jackson, whom he sustained, without ever wavering or doubting for a moment, in all his subsequent brilliant and exciting career. In the session of the legislature of 1837 and 1838 a bill was introduced by a democratic representative "for the extension of the right of suffrage," and was rejected—the democrats voting for it, and most of their opponents, of course, against it. A proposition was made at the same session for taking the votes for and against a convention to remodel the State constitution, which was also lost—the parties having divided upon that as upon its kindred project. During the next canvass for members of the legislature, these two propositions were the subjects for warm party discussion, more especially in the Ouachita senatorial district, where the candidates were Judge Morgan, a distinguished whig, who, as a representative in the other chamber, had voted against both bills, and General (then Major) Downs. The former, in his circular, justified his vote against the extension of the right of suffrage; while the latter, proclaiming his attachment to the principle in its broadest form, pledged himself to be willing to stand or fall by it and all its consequences. General Downs in this canvass also took ground in favor of a convention to reform the constitution of the State, and had the honor to be, I believe, the only senator elected wholly upon these two issues. The democratic representative, the candidate upon the same reform and extension of suffrage ticket, was also successful; thus revolutionizing the parish.

On the meeting of the legislature after this election, in compliance with his pledges, General Downs brought forward a bill for taking the sense of the good people of the State as to the necessity and expediency of calling a convention to amend the constitution, specifying in the body of the bill the following as the alterations more especially to be attained, viz:

"1st. That all judges shall be appointed for a limited period of years, and not for life.

"2d. That every free white male citizen of the United States, above the age of twenty-one years, and who shall have resided twelve months in the State, and six months in the parish in which he offers to vote, shall be entitled to a vote.

"3d. That a more equal and just system of representation, both in the senate and house of representatives, shall be adopted.

"4th. That sheriffs, coroners, constables, and other parish officers, be elected by the people.

"5th. That the governor be elected by the people alone, without the intervention of the legislature."

The bill having been referred to the committee on the judiciary, of which he was a member, was reported back without amendment, and sustained by a powerful report from his pen. This bill was defeated in the Senate by the casting-vote of the presiding officer—all the democrats proving its friends, and, with one exception, all their opponents its enemies. At the same time a similar bill was introduced in the other branch of the legislature by a democrat. There it shared a similar fate, but a single democrat voting against it. From this decision of the legislature, the democrats, under the leadership of General Downs, (whose powerful report had at once advanced him to the position of the first champion of the proposed reform,) appealed to the people in the canvass of 1840. In this struggle, so disastrous to the democracy, General Downs, who was conspicuously active, devoted himself throughout the canvass wholly to the prime duty of defending and advocating his principles with voice and pen. Though the State threw her vote for the federal candidate, and, as usual, elected a federal legislature, so deep had the principles of constitutional reform sunk into the public mind—thanks to the unceasing efforts of General Downs and his fellow-democratic speakers and writers—that, with the assistance of a few whigs pledged before the people to sustain this proposition to amend the constitution upon this vital question, he found himself in a majority on the meeting of the legislature.

His first move of the session of 1841 was again to bring forward his constitutional-reform proposition, making, as chairman of a select committee charged with its consideration, another elaborate report in its favor. In this document, after setting forth the difficulties thrown in the way of the consummation of the proposed reforms by the requirements of the existing constitution, under which, to succeed would be almost a miracle, General Downs triumphantly demonstrated the blighting influence upon the prosperity of Louisiana involved in the existence of features of the judiciary of the State worthy of the political darkness of the middle ages, and of the anti-democratic feature of exclusive (limited) suffrage then remaining upon the statute-book. He also attacked the principle of life-tenure of office, wherever found under the laws or constitution, with crushingly convincing force, and satisfied a vast majority of the people of the State that, in these and many other particulars, radical reforms were necessary in the civil polity of Louisiana, if they would ever hope for assistance from the laws in the enjoyment of their rights and the attainment of individual prosperity, such as they were fairly entitled to under proper institutions. Save the writings of Thomas Jefferson upon the dangers and embarrassments likely to grow out of the perpetuation in this country of veteran abuses in the law systems of Europe, I have met with no other so powerful exposition of the propriety of legal reforms. This paper, having served as a text for the advocates of reform in American State constitutions subsequently amended, will remain the guide to direct the labors of all in the United States who, desiring to live up to the spirit of the age, aim to effect changes in fundamental regulations, framed to suit society as it existed half a century since. The limits of this notice will not permit me to quote from this elaborate paper. Its eulogy, however, is to be found in the fidelity with which the principles it inculcates were insisted upon by the reformers returned to the conventions which have since remodelled the constitutions of not only Louisiana, but of Texas, Missouri, and New York.

Under the stunning effect of this report, the bill of General Downs passed the senate by the constitutional vote—a majority of all the members elected to the body. Unfortunately, the house, instead of immediately acting upon it, took a copy of the bill introduced by a member, which seriously endangered the consummation of the project, as, under the existing constitution, to authorize the submission of the question of a convention to the people, the bill for that purpose was required to be enacted by both houses within the first twenty days of the session. Commencing with a motion for postponement, (equivalent to a motion for its rejection,) the whigs in the house fought the bill at every step by proposing odious amendments, and other tricks of legislative diplomacy, which so often enable a minority to defeat the purposes of the majority. The bill was finally passed in a shape to give the convention a *carte blanche* to enact any and all needful constitutional reforms, without regard to its specifications; but at so late a period, that a legislative *coup de main* was necessary to secure its re-enactment by the senate within the constitutional term of twenty days. To this end, General Downs procured the suspension of a rule standing in the way of its consideration over a decision of the Chair against the motion. It was *passed* within the constitutional hour, and returned again to the house, the whig members of which body deserted their seats to break up the quorum usually required when bills were thus returned. This ruse, however, proved of no avail; for, as the friends of the bill soon made apparent, it had been *enacted* according to the forms required by the constitution, (which did not demand its engrossment within twenty days,) if not by the custom of the legislature. After a short struggle upon this unimportant technicality, the whigs abandoned the contest before the legislature, and prepared to meet the friends of reform before the people—the question being, Shall this convention be called or not? At the same session of the legislature, through the exertions of General Downs and his democratic fellow-members, a resolution for the extension of the suffrage to every free white male citizen of the United States above the age of twenty-one years passed the senate by the constitutional majority, and was laid on the table in the house—its friends, as before, being democrats with one or two exceptions, and its opponents all whigs.

On the 8th of January, 1842, the democrats of Louisiana met in New Orleans in State convention; and, nominating Governor Mouton as their candidate for governor, by resolutions and an address—both from the pen of General Downs, the most prominent member—they made the proposed reforms their issues of the approaching canvass. In this address General Downs formally incorporated the war on the banking system of the State, which he and other individual democrats had carried on since 1837, in the cycle of the measures of the democratic party.

Upon these issues the democracy triumphed—for the first time electing a majority of the legislature, and obtaining the order of the people for the assembling of the convention to revise and amend the constitution.

At the succeeding session of the legislature an election for members of the convention was ordered under the vote of the people above referred to, and in the memorable contest of 1844 they were chosen. Among them was—the life and soul of the movement—General S. W. Downs himself. As the whigs had opposed the proposition in its every stage, in this election they were badly beaten—a handsome majority of the members chosen being democrats, in favor of thorough and sweeping reforms.

On the 14th of January, 1845, this important body met in New Orleans, and sat *de die in diem* until the 16th of May following—full four months—both political parties having sent up their first men: it embraced, indeed, almost all the great and learned men of the State identified in any manner with public affairs. During the year previous to the meeting of this body General Downs had been elected a brigadier general—an office of responsibility and labor under the old constitution of Louisiana—and had served the State as a senator, and in the capacity of elector for President and Vice President; which, in the South, it will be remembered, requires a devotion of all the time and talent of the candidate for five or six months of the year in which residents of Louisiana avoid active bodily or mental exercise as dangerous to health. While engaged in the discharge of his duties as a member of the convention, he was honored with the unsolicited appointment of district attorney for the district of Louisiana by Mr. Polk. General Downs, however, did not qualify and enter upon the discharge of the duties of this office before seeing his hopes of radical constitutional reform crowned with success. The whigs opposed with vehement resistance almost all the reforms proposed, and more especially the proposition to place naturalized citizens in all respects on a footing with those of native birth. Upon this question, which was the subject of protracted debate, in which all the great minds of the convention participated, he and a few others delivered arguments of so much force—so conclusively demonstrating the impropriety of requiring a longer residence in the State to entitle *naturalized* citizens of the United States to the franchise than it was the intention of the convention to demand of the native-born—that without distinction of party the Europeans by birth, residents of New Orleans, presented them with an address and medals. I recur to this fact, because, in having occasion to denounce the tone of Mr. Gallatin's famous pamphlet against the Mexican war in a speech in the Senate of the United States, he took occasion to point out in strong terms the impropriety of an indulgence in aspersions upon the integrity and character of the United States government on the part of those naturalized citizens whose hearts, like that of Mr. Gallatin, are wrapped up in the systems of the European world. This portion of his famous speech (on the Mexican war) was garbled and misquoted by the federal press, with the design of creating an unfounded impression that his sympathies were with the Native-American party. This very characteristic federal trick, however, is so completely refuted by his previous labors to secure unimpaired and without delay all the rights of citizenship to the foreign-born, as promised in the legislation of the general government, that it is not necessary to be further noticed here.

But to resume the thread of my history. The constitution of Louisiana, as then existing, (which had been adopted in 1812,) was but a version of the old constitution of Kentucky, the imperfections of which gave rise to the embarrassments and the general bankruptcy of its citizens, ending in the never-to-be forgotten "old" and "new court" party troubles of that State, in which this charter was finally swept from their statute-books. The right of suffrage was restricted without reason or judgment. The judiciary were irresponsible, and held office for life. Of course, therefore, they were inefficient, tyrannical, and corrupt. The public expenditures were enormous, out of proportion to the means of the State, having really brought the treasury to bankruptcy, only concealed by issuing stock for an annually increasing State debt; the actual revenue falling short some $200,000 a year of meeting the public expenditures. To go to law to obtain one's rights was in fact to be well-nigh ruined, and getting a judgment, after long years of litigation, was to find one's adversary's property swamped in paying his own costs of the suit.

Among the important reforms effected by this convention was the extension of the right of suffrage, as advocated by General Downs when a candidate in 1838—"the adoption of the principle in its broadest form, and the voluntary assumption of all its consequences."

[Here follows in the original article an analysis of the new constitution of Louisiana, which is omitted.]

From these extracts, it will be perceived that there are far more of the doctrines of Thomas Jefferson infused in the new constitution of Louisiana than in that of any other State of the American Union. It certainly discovers more political foresight and insight, and more perfect reliance on the principles upon which popular governments are based, than are to be traced in any other series of these fundamental laws.

I need hardly pronounce the new constitution of Louisiana one of the best American State constitutions in existence; for this opinion will suggest itself to all who believe with the writer that the world is governed too much—one of the fundamental axioms of the creed of the Jeffersonian democrat. From the introduction of his first constitutional-reform proposition, in 1838, into the legislature, until the ratification of the new constitution, General Downs led the reformers, never ceasing for an instant in his labors, or wavering under the many and severe personal controversies in which they involved him.

While engaged upon this Herculean task, as before remarked, he had another in hand of scarcely less importance—more dangerous to himself, and requiring the exercise of severe exertions of his physical and mental powers. From 1838 to 1842 he was in the field against the banks of the State—sixteen in number. They were wholly irresponsible, and many of them insolvent, while they were encouraging among the people the spirit of individual business speculation and recklessness, (the existence of which alone enabled them to conceal their bankruptcy, so as in fact to control the fortunes of the people and the politics of the State.) General Downs, in performing his task, became a mark for the shafts of almost all the bank officers, orators, stockholders, debtors, attorneys, and writers in the State. The agents and supporters of these institutions in the legislature—men of eminent abilities and great weight of character—fought him at every step. Protesting their solvency, and denying his allegation that they maintained a fictitious vitality only by fraud and corruption, they yet refused him the demanded exposition of their affairs.

In January, 1842, he delivered his great speech (in the senate of Louisiana) against the banks, which is replete with a more powerful exposition of the thieving iniquity of Mr. Biddle's bank schemes and principles, and of the dangers, corruptions, and flagrant wrong involved in the existence of banking privileges, as usurped by the moneyed corporations of Louisiana, than is embraced in any other State paper to which the great Jackson contest against the power and corruption of the Bank of the United States gave rise—for this bank war in Louisiana was but a branch of the old Jackson anti-bank controversy. The banks of that State had suspended in 1837, and, resuming with Mr. Biddle, had again promptly followed his example in suspending in 1839. The bank bill of this session, which was indeed the old project of 1838, was designed, first to force these institutions to come under the control of the State, and next to make such expositions of their affairs as would enable the legislature to judge whether they had forfeited their charters, and the community to distinguish the solvent from the insolvent.

At this session the labors of Gen. Downs were crowned with such strong demonstrations of public opinion, that Governor Romain (a whig) and a handful of whig members came to his assistance, and thus carried through this important democratic project. Under the operations of this law the truth was soon told; for the consequent examination of the banks resulted in proving the hopless and fraudulent insolvency of eleven of the sixteen—all of which soon exploded, leaving but five in existence. To this day the five have continued sound. This irrefragable proof of the justice of the position so early taken, and sustained with so much courage and perseverance by General Downs in overwhelming the State bank party under a load of public odium, operated greatly to increase his previous popularity, and thus eventually to place him in his present enviable position.

Throughout the bank contest, as in that for the extension of the right of suffrage and constitutional reform, General Downs was the main mark for the shafts of the opposition, who levelled their missiles of destruction at his head as though impressed with the belief that in silencing him they would achieve the overthrow of this important purpose of the democracy. The democratic reader who has witnessed the struggle which combined and corrupt local banks made for the preservation of their privilege to plunder, when the rod of reform is uplifted against them, will understand that in this combat every possible scheme to defeat the final exposure was resorted to. Though aided in his good work by an almost unanimous democratic party, the chief labor and the weight of the federal odium fell upon General Downs. By way of illustrating his position in this contest, I here present the reader with two extracts from the federal papers of that day. The first is from the New Orleans Bee—then the principal organ of the banks of the State, edited by Mr. Bullit, who, on the 23d of June, 1849, was to commence the publication at Washington of the official organ of the general administration. The second is an extract from a letter in the Concordia Intelligencer—then, as since, the best conducted federal paper in the State. From these papers it will at once be perceived that General Downs was, indeed, the life and soul of the laborious task of reform the democrats of the legislature had in hand:

"The crisis.—The State senate.—The people.—The fiat has gone forth, and henceforward an abject, dumb, and servile submission to the imperial behests of the senate can alone protect the citizens from the denunciation, reproach, and slander of its inquisitor general. The press must be muzzled, the presidents and directors of our banks must violate the charters under which they act, and compromise the interests of their stockholders, in the indecent haste to prostrate themselves before the Jauggernaut that is to crush them. The citizen who refuses to abase himself before the standard of perfectibility set up by the senate is no longer entitled to the immunities or consideration of freemen. We venture to assert that the history of free government, from the dawn of liberty to this hour, does not furnish such an example of tyranny, usurpation, and scandalous disregard of the rights of the people, as has been exhibited by the upper branch of the legislature within the past month, unless, indeed, it be found in the legislation of South Carolina during the rebellion of 1832, when jurors, judges, constables, and militia officers were sworn on the Bible of nullification instead of the Holy Evangelist, before they could enter upon the discharge of their duties.

"The moving spirits in that body have assumed the powers of the executive, legislature, and judiciary. The executive nominated, according to law, certain directors for those banks in which the State had an interest. The senate held up the nominations until its bill had become a law, and forthwith passed a resolution inquiring of the nominees if they were opposed to the bank bill, and directing them to hand in their answers at a given hour. We would like to know when before, in the history of free government, was a step like this taken? And who can doubt, if a vacancy in the judiciary were to take place, that any one nominated by the governor for the office would be in like manner interrogated, and his opinion favorable to the constitutionality of the bank law made the *sine qua non* of this confirmation. The nominations of those persons sent to the senate as State directors, who refused to answer the resolution above noticed, were rejected. This is a novel tenure of office. They have already passed a law against the constitution, vacating the office of attorney general in case he does not, within ten days after a prescribed period, move against the banks ; thus assuming to themselves the power of impeachment vested in the house of representatives, and condemning, before accusation or trial, a high functionary under the constitution. There is but one step more to be taken ; and that is, to pass a resolution requiring the judges of the supreme court to hand in their opinions upon the constitutionality of the law, and procure the impeachment of those who refuse to respond or question its conformity with the constitution.

"The senate's finance committee have taken upon themselves the functions of inquisitors. They are not satisfied with encroaching upon the executive, but they must invade the judiciary. Their chairman, Mr. Downs, pronounces upon violations of law, and denounces the penalties against offenders, with as much *nonchalance* as if he were judge, jury, and sheriff. He seems ambitious of prying into every man's business, and enlightening the public upon everybody's indebtedness to the bank. He thinks the other departments of the government utterly useless. And, indeed, the senate itself comes in for no better share of his esteem, the 'committee on finance' being alone capable of executing all the functions of government ; and, to simplify the system yet further, the chairman of the committee is fully competent to dispense with the assistance of his coadjutors. The whole theory, practice, and power of the government is reduced to a song—'*All in the Downs.*' "

In the senate, those members who were obviously the prominent men are Downs, Hoa, Sparrow, and Walker.

"Major Downs is a native of Tennessee, now about forty years of age, and in the prime vigor of his physical and intellectual powers. He has been six years a member of the senate, and in that time has gained the reputation and character of a leader of his party in the State senate. His politics are democratic, and those principles blend with nearly all his legislative efforts. In debate he is free, open, manly, and candid, and enters with so much spirit and earnestness into his subject as to inspire confidence in his sincerity. Indeed, it will require time for the observer to discover the discipline with which he has prepared himself for success, so candid and fair does he seem in discussion; yet it is probable that no member of the senate drills his intellectual forces with more rigor for success at all hazards. When the conflict unexpectedly becomes difficult and doubtful, he becomes aroused, is somewhat thrown off his guard, and the weak points of his defence, if any there be, are developed. His strong prejudices are his greatest failing. Few have ever heard him yield a point; for he can defend, with considerable array of truth, and a tremendous cannonade of blank cartridges after his effective ammunition is exhausted, any position which he assumes. He considers the principles of his political creed a sacred depository, which he is bound to guard from the attacks of the enemy's regular assault in line, as well as from the insidious and skirmishing sorties of scouting debate; and he will command all his forces to charge with the same desperation upon a wandering whig militia-man as upon the solid column of truth and justice, making good way to the citadel of democracy. He is a valiant soldier in the ranks of his party, and never loses an opportunity to fight. The course taken by Major Downs in reference to the banks and bank laws has rendered him very unpopular in the city—with what degree of justice remains to be seen; for no one now seems able to guess what will be the ultimate effects of this strange and complicated fabric of legislative manufacture," (referring to the bank law urged by General Downs.) * * * * * "Nature blessed him with a strong mind, strong body, decision of character, even to stubbornness. In the social relations of life he is much esteemed as a hospitable, temperate, and intellectual man. His stature is tall, but inelegant; his complexion dark; hair black; eyes blue; and, taken all in all, is a very hard-favored man."

If the measures to compass the reform taken by General Downs were arbitrary, and involved the assumption of unlawful authority, as alleged in the article from "The Bee," their triumphant justification is to be found in the fact that he was dealing with corrupt institutions, then *above all law*, almost wholly irresponsible, as the equally corrupt and bank-influenced judiciary of the State at that time had decided. Dangerous diseases at times require desperate remedies, such as the Bee argues was resorted to. The final disclosure of the true condition of these institutions relieved General Downs of the "odium" which his measures had generated against him—that is, in the estimation of all the community whose good opinion was desirable to a man of true integrity.

But I must hasten on. The blow-up of the insolvent banks of the State greatly strengthened the democratic party—demonstrating the patriotism of its warfare of five or six years' duration. Indeed, that event secured a triumph for the democracy for the first time in the State election soon following.

In the spring of 1844 General Downs was chosen to be a delegate for the State at large in the Baltimore Convention, and instructed to support Mr. Van Buren. He was at the same time nominated a candidate for presidential elector by the democratic State convention.

On the promulgation of the anti-Texas letter of Mr. Van Buren, which took place after these nominations were made, General Downs promptly threw them up, alleging that he could not support a traitor to the principles of democracy and the South. But after Mr. Polk was nominated, at the request of the State central committee, he resumed his position as a candidate for elector. In the discharge of his duty as a candidate for elector, on the 19th of June, 1844, he delivered, at Farmersville, in the parish of Union, the most elaborate, carefully prepared, and powerful argument in favor of the annexation of Texas which, as far as my reading extends, the canvass produced. This was at once printed in large numbers by the democracy, and sent in every direction over the Southwest, furnishing the speakers and writers of our party with by far the most extensive and convincing collection of "proof from the record" brought to bear in favor of that great measure of the democracy. As before remarked, he was chosen an elector, and voted for James K. Polk.

On the occurrence of the first vacancy from Louisiana in the United States Senate, after the election of 1844, General Downs, without solicitation, was unanimously nominated by the democratic members of the legislature, and triumphantly elected to that honorable post, in which his career has been marked by quiet labor and retiring modesty. He has, however, in Washington, added not a little to his previous fame as a distinguished statesmen. As chairman of the Senate's Committee on Private Land Claims, his indefatigable habits and extensive legal attainments have been of great service in obtaining for honest claimants their dues, and guarding the public treasury against unjust demands. As one of the Judiciary Committee, to whom was referred the bill of Senator Douglas for the admission of California as a State, he made a minority report, dissenting from the views of his fellow committee men upon the question of the constitutionality of the famous proposition of Mr. Douglas, and reviewing and refuting the positions of that paper *seriatim*. It will be recollected that the majority report, drawn up by Mr. Berrien, denying the constitutionality of the proposed measure, went on to argue from the history of the action of this government in the admission of all the new States, by way of sustaining this view. General Downs attacked these positions at the root, showing that in this case Congress had been asked to do no more than it had in fact, at a prior date, done virtually in the case of Vermont and in that of Kentucky. The latter, when admitted, had no State constitution framed, nor indeed for fourteen months after; and as for laws, she was then entirely without them—being in a chaotic state.

His triumphant refutation of the facts presented by the majority, and consequently of the conclusions drawn from these facts, made converts of a sufficient number of senators to render it apparent that a majority stood ready to enact some bill on the principles of that of Mr. Douglas, when satisfied that it could pass the other branch of Congress.

The speech of Senator Downs on the "ten-regiment bill" was regarded by Congress, without distinction of party, as perhaps the most conclusive defence of the war policy and measures of the administration to which that memorble debate gave rise. This paper—for it was an elaborate State paper—embraced the result of long labor, close investigation, and profound thought upon the subject-matters being considered. Yet young for his position, and in the possession of all his powers in full vigor, Senator Downs bids fair to win a broadly national reputation in the war which special privilege is destined to wage, for the next three or four years, against the rights of the States and the people of the States, under the auspices of the federal administration of the general government. He can hardly fail to have in the Senate of the United States, in all that time, a field suited to render his peculiar talents and attainments almost of as much value to the Union at large as they have been to the people of Louisiana within the period particularly reviewed in this sketch. Knowing the character of his mind, his abilities, and attainments, and the history of his previous labors in behalf of sound republican progress, and also anticipating the efforts which federalism will essay in the legislation of the next Congress to take advantage of the election of President

Taylor, the writer, in conclusion, predicts, if spared by Providence to his country, he will come to be regarded as perhaps the main senatorial bulwark of the democratic party in future contests over principles and measures in which the supremacy of Thomas Jefferson's readings of law or rights may be involved. I cannot close this sketch without noticing the fate of the classmates of General Downs when under the tuition of the Rev. Mr. Craighead, mentioned previously; for their story, full of vicissitudes and sorrow, illustrates the state of society and of the times in which General Downs persevered in his labors for reform until they were crowned with triumphant success. Of the seven, *five* are already in the grave.

Winn died at the close of 1840, a victim to fatigue and exposure in the presidential campaign, and chagrin at the defeat of Mr. Van Buren. Frederick Guion fell in a duel at Natchez. One of the Whartons lost his life in the accidental discharge of a pistol; the other died from a wound received at the battle of San Jacinto. Bosworth, who since died in the service of his country in the Mexican war, had his right arm shattered to pieces in a furious rencontre; and General Downs himself was shot through the lungs by a musket ball in a duel. Yet there was not one among them not remarkable for suavity of disposition.

The portion of this sketch which precedes was written and published in June, 1849. There remains to be added, to bring down the record to the present time, a brief review of the course of Senator Downs on the compromise measures of 1850. Few men acted a more conspicuous part, or had greater influence in bringing to a satisfactory and safe result those important, exciting, and dangerous questions, than he. No member of the Thirty-first Congress, or other statesman of the nation, has less to regret in his past action on them—none whose course will better stand the test of time, the ordeal of all human action, or has received, and will continue to receive, a greater share of the approbation of all good men and true patriots of all sections. His course on this subject is a part of the history of his country, and requires no extended comment here. It may be stated in a few words. As a cotton planter, largely interested in slave property, and a senator from a State more largely interested in it, in proportion to her population, than any other State, he strongly, and with great ability and success, opposed the Wilmot proviso, the abolition of slavery in the District of Columbia, and the slave trade between the States—the assaults which the South had chiefly to contend against. He advocated, and was an active member of the Compromise Committee of Thirteen, sustaining the report of the committee, though it did not come up to his views in all respects, because it contained none of the measures injurious to the South mentioned above, and benefited it by the fugitive-slave bill and the Texas compromise. He acted cheerfully with men of all parties and sections on these measures; but in doing so he did not cease to be a democrat, and when they where consummated, or while they were pending, refused to enter into any new organizations of Union or State-rights parties—insisting that they (the compromise measures) are in accordance with the old democratic doctrines and the doctrines of Jefferson, Jackson, and Polk, and required no new creed or combination to settle them. His course was triumphantly sustained by the people of his own State and the South generally; for all the States of the South now acquiesce in the Compromise, as well as nearly all the statesmen who once opposed it; and the course of no southern member of Congress who took a prominent part in the great contest is so generally applauded and approved by the sound democrats of the North as his. There is, therefore, no objection to him North or South on this ground. Is not this a strong reason why he should be taken up as a candidate for the Vice Presidency, if the President is to be from the North, as will no doubt be the case? Another reason might be stated in favor of running him for this place. Louisiana is a doubtful State; the vote will be a close one. It is strongly in favor of union and the Compromise. General Downs would give the ticket a strength there which no other man would. This is admitted by all in that State. In the late election of senator in that State he received every democratic vote, Union and State-rights men, and three whig votes; and the people are indignant at many of the whig members of the legislature because they did not vote for him as was expected. Either General Scott or Mr. Fillmore will be the whig candidate. If Scott should be the man, with his doubtful position on the slavery question, the contrast of the democratic ticket, with Downs on it, would help our cause. If Fillmore should be the whig candidate, still more important would it be to have a man on our ticket as much identified with the Compromise as he is, or more so. General Williamson, a prominent State-rights member of the legislature, nominated him in the caucus for senator—so he would be cheerfully supported by democrats holding similar opinions. The nature of General Downs's public services heretofore has been calculated to give him peculiar qualifications for the office of Vice President and President of the Senate. At the end of his present term he will have served thirteen years in the *Senate*—State and federal.

www.ingramcontent.com/pod-product-compliance
Lightning Source LLC
LaVergne TN
LVHW020639110826
845149LV00004B/1278

9781418190040